W9-AAJ-438

JOBS KIDS WANT

WHAT'S IT REALLY LIKE TO BE A CARPENTER?

CHRISTINE HONDERS

PowerKiDS press.
New York

Published in 2020 by The Rosen Publishing Group, Inc.
29 East 21st Street, New York, NY 10010

First Edition

Editor: Greg Roza
Book Design: Michael Flynn

Photo Credits: Cover, p. 1 Fh Photo/Shutterstock.com; pp. 4, 6, 8, 10, 12, 14, 16, 18, 20, 22 (background) Apostrophe/Shutterstock.com; p. 5 goodluz/Shutterstock.com; p. 7 pikselstock/Shutterstock.com; p. 9 Dirk Saeger/Shutterstock.com; p. 11 Thomas Barrat/Shutterstock.com; p. 13 Pressmaster/Shutterstock.com; p. 15 UfaBizPhoto/Shutterstock.com; p. 17 Steve Debenport/E+/Getty Images; p. 19 gualtiero boffi/Shutterstock.com; p. 21 p_ponomareva/Shutterstock.com; p. 22 Mega Pixel/Shutterstock.com.

Cataloging-in-Publication Data

Names: Honders, Christine.
Title: What's it really like to be a carpenter? / Christine Honders.
Description: New York : PowerKids Press, 2020. | Series: Jobs kids want | Includes glossary and index.
Identifiers: ISBN 9781538349762 (pbk.) | ISBN 9781538349786 (library bound) | ISBN 9781538349779 (6 pack)
Subjects: LCSH: Carpentry–Vocational guidance–Juvenile literature. | Carpenters–Juvenile literature.
Classification: LCC TH5608.8 H66 2020 | DDC 694.023–dc23

Manufactured in the United States of America

CPSIA Compliance Information: Batch #CSPK19. For Further Information contact Rosen Publishing, New York, New York at 1-800-237-9932.

CONTENTS

Builders and Fixers

Lots of kids want to be teachers, police officers, or doctors when they grow up. What about the people who build schools, police stations, and hospitals? Carpenters build and fix things made of wood. They make things we use every day.

What Carpenters Do

Carpenters cut pieces of wood and put them together to make objects, such as furniture and cabinets. Sometimes they work on large projects, such as houses or bridges. Carpenters are **skilled** at working with their hands and use many different tools. They are also good at math.

Carpenters of the Past

Carpenters have been around for thousands of years! Early humans used stones to shape wooden tools. Later people used metal tools to build wooden furniture and buildings. The Vikings made large, strong, wooden ships. They used these ships to travel to new lands.

Viking
shipbuilding tools

Carpenters Today

Carpenters are still an important part of our **community**. They help build new homes and businesses. Some carpenters build frames that can be filled with other building supplies, such as **concrete**. New **technology** helps them create new things and work faster.

Training to Be a Carpenter

Future carpenters take math classes in high school. Then, they get carpentry training at college or technical school. Students must work for a few years as an **apprentice**. They also need to pass a safety course before they're able to work as carpenters.

What You Need to Know

Carpenters know how to cut and shape wood. They also know the best kind of wood for each project. Carpenters are good at math. They use math to figure out how much wood they need. They measure wood using rulers. They **calculate** how much wood is needed for a job.

What Else Does It Take?

Carpenters know how to read **blueprints**. They're able to use power tools, hammers, and saws. Carpenters who work on big projects must work well with others. They follow the safety rules and use gear, such as goggles and hard hats.

Why Carpenters Are Important

Lots of people can create things on computers. But carpenters know how to build things with their hands. We need carpenters to help bring our ideas to life. Carpenters also help fix broken things. If carpenters keep building, our world will keep growing!

Working Hard and Feeling Good

Carpentry can be a hard job. But most carpenters like their jobs. They feel proud when a project is finished. Carpenters use their skills to make their own lives better. Knowing how to fix things yourself makes you feel good!

Carpenters Wanted!

We'll always need carpenters to build newer, stronger buildings. Some carpenters repair old bridges and tunnels. Others use their hands to create beautiful art. Our world changes every day. We need carpenters to build the things that make it a better place.

GLOSSARY

apprentice: A student who works with an experienced person to get training in a job.

blueprint: A plan for a building that workers follow.

calculate: To figure out by using math.

community: The people living in an area.

concrete: A hardened mixture of sand, water, broken stone, and other materials used in construction.

skilled: Having the knowledge needed to complete a task or job.

technology: The use of science to solve problems.

INDEX

WEBSITES

Due to the changing nature of Internet links, PowerKids Press has developed an online list of websites related to the subject of this book. This site is updated regularly. Please use this link to access the list: www.powerkidslinks.com/JKW/carpenter